RELIGION AND
FREE SPEECH

BY MICHAEL CAPEK

CONTENT CONSULTANT

Chad W. Flanders
Associate Professor
Saint Louis University School of Law

Essential Library
An Imprint of Abdo Publishing | abdopublishing.com

Published by Abdo Publishing, a division of ABDO, PO Box 398166, Minneapolis, Minnesota 55439. Copyright © 2016 by Abdo Consulting Group, Inc. International copyrights reserved in all countries. No part of this book may be reproduced in any form without written permission from the publisher. Essential Library™ is a trademark and logo of Abdo Publishing.

Printed in the United States of America, North Mankato, Minnesota
092015
012016

THIS BOOK CONTAINS
RECYCLED MATERIALS

Cover Photo: Britta Pedersen/Picture-Alliance/DPA/AP Images
Interior Photos: Marcus Golejewski/Geisler-Fotopr/Picture-Alliance/DPA/AP Images, 4–5; Mirwais Rahmani/AP Images, 7; Andres Kudacki/AP Images, 11; North Wind Picture Archives, 14–15; SuperStock/Glow Images, 17; Eric Draper/White House/AP Images, 22; LM Otero/AP Images, 25; Bettmann/Corbis, 26–27, 34, 68, 80, 91; AP Images, 30, 82; Bill Clark/Roll Call/Getty Images, 37; Martin Wimmer/iStockphoto, 38–39; Gerald Herbert/AP Images, 41; Sandy Huffaker/Corbis, 45; iStockphoto, 49, 74–75, 88–89; Ron Sachs/Picture-Alliance/DPA/AP Images, 50–51; Matthew Hinton/AP Images, 54; Michael Conroy/AP Images, 57; The' N. Pham/The Virginian-Pilot/AP Images, 58; Brent Drinkut/Statesman-Journal/AP Images, 61; Rusty Schramm/Temple Daily Telegram/AP Images, 62–63; Cheryl Casey/Shutterstock Images, 71; Julia Margaret Cameron/Library of Congress, 76; Jim West/ImageBroker RM/Glow Images, 86; Catherine Yeulet/iStockphoto/Thinkstock, 94; Ng Han Guan/AP Images, 96

Editor: Melissa York
Series Designer: Maggie Villaume

Library of Congress Control Number: 2015944930

Cataloging-in-Publication Data

Capek, Michael.
 Religion and free speech / Michael Capek.
   p. cm. -- (Special reports)
ISBN 978-1-62403-902-7 (lib. bdg.)
Includes bibliographical references and index.
1. Civil rights--Juvenile literature. 2. Human rights--Juvenile literature. I. Title.
323--dc23

                                                    2015944930

CONTENTS

CHAPTER ONE

ALWAYS A
RIGHT?

O n the morning of January 7, 2015, a small black car pulled up outside the offices of *Charlie Hebdo*, a well-known humor magazine in Paris, France. Two masked gunmen, dressed in black and armed with assault rifles, got out and entered the building. Inside, they asked a maintenance man sitting at a reception desk where the *Charlie Hebdo* offices were. As soon as the man told them, they shot him.

Upstairs, at the entrance to the magazine's main offices, the gunmen forced a staff member to open the door, which was always kept securely locked. A number of *Charlie Hebdo*'s writers and cartoonists had received death threats from people and groups that objected to pictures and words that had appeared in the magazine.

People worldwide attended vigils mourning the *Charlie Hebdo* victims and affirming their support for free speech.

"FREE-SPEECH ABSOLUTISTS'
INSISTENCE ON THE RIGHT TO
OFFEND, TO SAY AND WRITE
OFFENSIVE AND PROFANE THINGS,
ALONG WITH THE RIGHT TO
BLASPHEME, HAS CREATED AN
ENVIRONMENT, A CULTURE-SCAPE,
IN WHICH LITTLE IS HELD DEAR
OR BEAUTIFUL AND ALMOST
NOTHING IS SACRED. AND WE,
THE INSTIGATORS, ARE THE
LOSERS FOR IT, DEPLETED
SPIRITUALLY."[1]

**—WRITER AND PLAYWRIGHT CARLA
SEAQUIST, 2015**

The cartoons and writing that regularly appeared in *Charlie Hebdo* were extreme by anyone's standards. Many people thought the magazine went too far in its attempts to make fun of religion, politics, and a wide variety of social issues. Satire was one thing, but *Charlie Hebdo* was frequently vulgar and even obscene.

Too bad, the magazine's cartoonists and writers often said. France had strong free speech laws, and they were simply exercising them fully. Besides, the French were known for their irreverent sense of humor, and many people bought and enjoyed the scandalous magazine.

Yet, not everyone was amused. The most serious and frequent threats over the past few years had come from certain Islamic organizations that were angry mostly over cartoons depicting the Prophet Muhammad. While most Muslims do not react violently, they traditionally object

Cartoons published in *Charlie Hebdo* have routinely sparked protest in Islamic countries.

to the display of any picture of their holy prophet as irreverent or sacrilegious. Some extreme groups consider it blasphemy, a criminally irreverent act punishable by death. *Charlie*'s artists and writers understood this but ignored threats and kept publishing these depictions.

The masked gunmen who arrived on the morning of January 7 were there to perform what they saw as their religious duty. Once inside the magazine's main offices, they found a staff meeting in progress. They opened fire, killing a police bodyguard. Then they began asking for various staff members by name, killing editor Stephane Charbonnier and four others in rapid order. Next, they killed three other staff members and a visitor. Witnesses later reported hearing the gunmen shout, "We have avenged the Prophet Muhammad" and "God is Great" in Arabic as they named and shot the journalists.[2]

The attackers fled. After a massive manhunt and more shootings that brought the death toll to 17, the gunmen were finally tracked down and killed in a shootout with police. They were later identified as two Muslim French brothers with ties to the international terrorist organization al-Qaeda. In a separate, and presumably connected, incident, security forces killed another Muslim man after he shot and killed several people at a Jewish market in Paris. This attack, too, appeared to be religiously motivated, since the gunman had connections to ISIS, an Islamic extremist group that controls territory in Iraq and Syria and has vowed to destroy the United States and Israel.

REACTING TO THE VIOLENCE

The world reacted in various ways to the Paris attacks. The most noticeable were demonstrations of grief, shock, and support in cities all across Europe. In France alone,

MORE TO THE
STORY

OTHER ATTACKS

The *Charlie Hebdo* attacks in Paris are not an isolated incident. Islamic fury over any depiction of the Prophet Muhammad has sparked deadly attacks before. In 2005, Denmark's largest newspaper, *Jyllands-Posten*, published cartoons of Muhammad. Muslims around the globe protested. The newspaper and the cartoonists who drew the images began receiving death threats. In 2008, when terrorists attempted to kill one of the cartoonists, 17 other Danish newspapers published the cartoons as a free speech demonstration.

On February 14, 2015, a lone gunman wearing a Muslim head covering opened fire in a café in Copenhagen where a public discussion, *Art, Blasphemy, and Freedom of Expression*, was taking place. One of the speakers was a Swedish cartoonist, Lars Vilks, who published a cartoon in 2007 of the Prophet Muhammad as a dog. Vilks was not injured in the attack, but one person was killed and three others were wounded before police shot and killed the gunman.

Media outlets in Denmark and other nations have been rethinking publishing the same or similar cartoons. After the *Charlie Hebdo* attacks, *Jyllands-Posten* decided not to join other newspapers that reprinted the French magazine's cartoons. An editorial in the newspaper explained why. "We have lived with the fear of a terrorist attack for nine years, and yes, that is the explanation why we are not reprinting the cartoons. . . . We are also aware that we are therefore bowing to violence and intimidation."[3]

"IN FRANCE, WE ALWAYS HAVE THE RIGHT TO WRITE AND DRAW. AND IF SOME PEOPLE ARE NOT HAPPY WITH THIS, THEY CAN SUE US, AND WE CAN DEFEND OURSELVES. THAT'S DEMOCRACY. YOU DON'T THROW BOMBS, YOU DISCUSS, YOU DEBATE. BUT YOU DON'T ACT VIOLENTLY. WE HAVE TO STAND AND RESIST PRESSURE FROM EXTREMISM."[5]

—LAURENT LÉGER FOR *CHARLIE HEBDO*, 2012

3.7 million people joined with visitors from all over the world, including the leaders of many nations, in marches defying terrorism and supporting free speech. Many carried signs that said simply, "Je suis Charlie" (I am Charlie).[4] Surviving staff members at *Charlie Hebdo* vowed to publish the next issue, which they did. That issue featured a cartoon image of the Prophet Muhammad on the front. Many French Muslims marched, too, to remind the world most followers of their religion do not believe in violence and terror.

Official statements by the leaders of Muslim nations mostly denounced the attack. But some also blamed *Charlie Hebdo* for abusing its right to free speech. Iran's official media outlet noted such behavior harmed ongoing efforts by Islamic and non-Islamic nations to find a way to deal peacefully with one another. A Muslim media outlet said the Paris attacks should be seen as "an alarm bell for those who have in the past insulted Islam and the Prophet."[6] Yemen's president, Abed Rabbu Mansour Hadi has said much the same thing: "There should be limits for the freedom of expression, especially if such freedom blasphemes the beliefs of nations and defames their figures."[7]

Many people, both Muslims and non-Muslims, see the underlying issue as one of responsibility. After all, just because one has the right to speak, does that mean a person always *should*? If one uses hurtful, hateful

Marchers from the Islamic community reminded the world that most Muslims are not terrorists.

ATTACKS IN THE UNITED STATES

A group called the American Freedom Defense Initiative (AFDI) sponsored a so-called free speech art exhibit on May 2015, near Dallas, Texas, that featured a contest offering $10,000 for the best cartoon of the Prophet Muhammad.[8] The Southern Poverty Law Center, a civil rights group that keeps track of extreme groups in the United States, has called the AFDI a "hate group."[9] During the event, two heavily armed gunmen attempted to enter the arena where the event was being held. They were immediately shot and killed by a police guard at the entrance, who was the only other person injured in the attack.

The event's organizers have a long history of attacking Islamic beliefs and Muslim extremists. They said they wanted to make a stand for free speech following the *Charlie Hebdo* incident. The two gunmen were Muslims who had been under investigation by the FBI for possible terrorist activities.

language, or "fighting words," shouldn't one expect a violent reaction? Particularly if the speaker knows for sure that certain words or actions will result in a bad outcome, doesn't he have a responsibility to weigh his words carefully? Shouldn't he consider what harm his words or actions might cause innocent people before he says them?

Exactly this point was the outcome of the 1919 Supreme Court case of *Schenck v. United States*. The case had to do with the free speech rights of antiwar activists during World War I (1914–1918), who distributed leaflets encouraging young men to resist being drafted. Since the language of the pamphlets encouraged people to break the law and at the same time harmed

America's war effort, the speech was ruled dangerous and disruptive. In his ruling in this case, Justice Oliver Wendell Holmes wrote:

> The most stringent protection of free speech would not protect a man falsely shouting fire in a theater and causing a panic. . . . The question in every case is whether the words used are used in such circumstances and are of such a nature as to create a clear and present danger that they will bring about the substantive evils that Congress has a right to prevent.[10]

The metaphor Justice Holmes used in his ruling became a legal catchphrase in innumerable cases over the years. After all, in a crowded nation and world, filled with diverse political and religious opinions, what good comes from carelessly shouting "Fire!"?

FIGHTING WORDS

A police officer orders an angry demonstrator to move from a busy public sidewalk. The protester spouts obscene language at the officer and is arrested for disorderly conduct. He sues, claiming his First Amendment free speech rights were violated. His lawyer argues that prior cases have established that a person is free to speak, even if the content and message of his words are offensive.

This situation was the basis for a 1942 Supreme Court case, *Chaplinsky v. State of New Hampshire*. In its ruling, the court stated there are some types of speech that cannot be protected under the Constitution. "These include the lewd and obscene, the profane, the libelous, and the insulting, or 'fighting' words—those which by their very utterance inflict injury or tend to incite an immediate breach of the peace."[11]

CHAPTER TWO

THE ROOTS OF FREEDOM IN AMERICA

E uropean settlers escaping religious and political tyranny in their home countries began the American experiment. The idea of democratic freedom was not born in America. The general concept of civil rights, such as freedom of religion and speech, began in ancient Greece and Rome. Those ancient ideas, modified and codified in the US Constitution, sparked a worldwide revolution. Fittingly, ideas that began in ancient Europe returned to inspire modern nations founded upon the natural, inalienable, and fundamental rights of free people everywhere.

The Puritans were one early religious group that came to America to escape religious persecution.

"THE LEGITIMATE POWERS OF
GOVERNMENT EXTEND TO SUCH
ACTS ONLY AS ARE INJURIOUS
TO OTHERS. BUT IT DOES ME NO
INJURY FOR MY NEIGHBOR TO
SAY THERE ARE TWENTY GODS,
OR NO GOD. IT NEITHER PICKS MY
POCKET NOR BREAKS MY LEG."[2]

—THOMAS JEFFERSON, 1787

The early American colonists came from a wide variety of religious backgrounds. They were Catholics, Protestants, and any number of minor sects and groups. But many shared a common, fearful past of persecution, imprisonment, and even death. On the new, sprawling North American continent, they vowed to reclaim the precious liberties they had been denied by kings or governors in the old world—especially the freedom to worship as they saw fit. The early settlers understood the denial of that one fundamental right had automatically insured the loss of other "inalienable rights," such as the right to speak and assemble freely.[1]

Inspired by their determination to learn from past errors, they embarked on a bold experiment. They created a new nation based on a social contract—the assumption that a people can live together in peace and freedom if they willingly agree to give up a few less-important freedoms in order to ensure the most important ones. To do this, they had to create and give total power to a system of government that did not recognize or establish any particular religion or church. It required a great leap of faith—not just faith in religious leaders and elected governmental officials, but faith that the Constitution, a set of laws, would protect everyone equally and fairly.

The members of the Constitutional Convention understood the language of the document was all-important. Presided over by General George Washington, the convention met in Philadelphia in the summer of 1787. There, Alexander Hamilton, James

Thomas Jefferson's views about the separation of church and state and his push for the Bill of Rights shaped the Constitution although he did not attend the convention.

Madison, Robert Morris, and dozens of other statesmen wrestled with and argued about words and ideas that would guide the nation for generations to come. They could not agree, and many times tempers, ideals, and egos clashed with such fury they wondered how a peaceful, united nation could ever emerge from such chaos.

In 1789, the new Constitution came into effect, even though few of those who had framed the document believed it would stand the test of time. Its language seemed too vague, and the balance it called for between various components of the government and society seemed overly hopeful and idealistic. Indeed, the document did not appear to set in motion the machinery that would establish the "more perfect union" the Preamble to the Constitution called for. Yet, as James Madison, one of the principal writers of the Constitution, said at the time, no government can be perfect, and perhaps, "that which is the least imperfect is therefore the best government."[3] Because our government was "imperfect," the framers of the Constitution saw fit to leave room for future generations to interpret its meaning, to make it more perfect. The words had to be specific enough to provide guidelines for people to follow, yet vague enough to ensure the laws would apply to any number of different circumstances. Courts have done exactly that ever since—they constantly interpret the Constitution and apply it to situations and events no one in 1791 could possibly have envisioned.

The wording of the Constitution is vitally important: "Congress shall make no law respecting an establishment of religion, or prohibiting the free exercise thereof; or abridging the freedom of speech, or of the press; or the right of the people peaceably to assemble, and to petition the government for a redress of grievances."[4] The first

THE BATTLE OVER THE BILL OF RIGHTS

In 1787, the new American nation was in turmoil. The 1781 Articles of Confederation describing how the nation would be governed were simply not strong or specific enough. A Constitutional Convention made up of representatives from the 13 states met in Philadelphia, Pennsylvania, to write a new constitution. A battle quickly began between two opposing sides. The Federalists, headed by James Monroe, James Madison, and Thomas Jefferson, wanted a constitution that gave power to a strong national government. They did not believe it was necessary to spell out what rights Americans would have. Anti-Federalists, such as Patrick Henry and Samuel Adams, wanted a document that would control federal powers and protect state and individual rights. They demanded a specific list in the new constitution, a Bill of Rights.

The debate that went on during 1787 and 1788 was often bitter and angry. The battle ended and the new constitution was ratified only after delegates agreed that additions, or amendments, could be made to the document by a vote of Congress. The first ten of these amendments, which went into effect in 1791, were the Bill of Rights.

words have become known as "the establishment clause." This guarantees the government can never establish one religion as an official state religion or promote the importance of any particular religion over another. The second set of words, the "free exercise" clause, limits the government's power to interfere with an individual's choice or practice of religion. Next is the clause that prohibits the government from restricting or "abridging the freedom of speech," as well as freedoms of the press, petition, and assembly.

"BELIEVING WITH YOU THAT RELIGION IS A MATTER WHICH LIES SOLELY BETWEEN MAN & HIS GOD . . . THAT THE LEGITIMATE POWERS OF GOVERNMENT REACH ACTIONS ONLY, & NOT OPINIONS . . . [THE] LEGISLATURE SHOULD 'MAKE NO LAW RESPECTING AN ESTABLISHMENT OF RELIGION, OR PROHIBITING THE FREE EXERCISE THEREOF,' THUS BUILDING A WALL OF SEPARATION BETWEEN CHURCH & STATE."[5]

—PRESIDENT THOMAS JEFFERSON, "LETTER TO THE DANBURY BAPTISTS," 1802

AMERICA'S CIVIL RELIGION

Despite the constitutional barrier created between church and state, many people have argued over the years that the threads of Christianity are woven throughout American government, and that it may, in fact, be considered the United States' national religion. After all, today the US government proclaims, "in God We Trust" on its money. Millions of schoolchildren recite the words "under God" in the pledge to the American flag. For the past 200 years, sessions of the US Senate have opened with prayer, led by a government-appointed chaplain. Sessions of the US Supreme Court begin with the words, "God save the United States and this Honorable Court."[6] By tradition, American presidents take their inaugural Oath of Office by placing one hand upon the Bible and reciting the words, "So help me God."[7]

Throughout history, the language of US leaders has always been routinely religious. Prayer and other specific religious practices were considered not only acceptable, but also highly important in conducting governmental

"THE 'ESTABLISHMENT OF RELIGION' CLAUSE OF THE FIRST AMENDMENT MEANS AT LEAST THIS: NEITHER A STATE NOR THE FEDERAL GOVERNMENT CAN SET UP A CHURCH. NEITHER CAN PASS LAWS WHICH AID ONE RELIGION, AID ALL RELIGIONS, OR PREFER ONE RELIGION TO ANOTHER. . . . IN THE WORDS OF JEFFERSON, THE [FIRST AMENDMENT] CLAUSE AGAINST ESTABLISHMENT OF RELIGION BY LAW WAS INTENDED TO ERECT 'A WALL OF SEPARATION BETWEEN CHURCH AND STATE.' . . . THAT WALL MUST BE KEPT HIGH AND IMPREGNABLE."[8]

—JUSTICE HUGO BLACK, IN THE 1947 *EVERSON V. BOARD* OF EDUCATION RULING business. In his farewell speech to his troops in September 1796, George Washington called religion "a necessary spring of popular government."[9] Even in modern times, presidents and other politicians routinely use religious language, particularly in times of celebration or national crises. For example, after the deadly September 11, 2001, attacks on the World Trade Center, President George W. Bush led a national day of prayer and spoke at a prayer service at the Washington National Cathedral.

So how does a nation that claims in its Constitution that church and state must be kept separate justify such religious references? One answer may be, as one scholar

President George W. Bush participated in religious ceremonies commemorating the September 11, 2001, attacks.

has suggested, that these things are just "a vestige of the de facto religious establishment of the nineteenth century."[10] Similar to the national seal, motto, and flag, certain rituals and ways of speaking have become traditions, patriotic customs that link us to our past. They are evidence of what sociologist Robert Bellah calls an "American civil religion." This refers to a system or set of values and morals that all Americans believe in and hold dear, rather than the establishment of a particular "state religion."[11]

But even this explanation creates problems. After all, followers of some religions, such as Wiccans and Buddhists, do not worship or believe in the Judeo-Christian god. And atheists do not believe in any god at all. These groups have sometimes objected to forms and expressions that force them to speak and behave in ways that offend their beliefs. So, the question remains: How does the First Amendment protect the rights of all Americans? Courts, religious groups, and free speech activists continue debating the issues, searching for an answer that satisfies everyone.

FROM THE HEADLINES

THE RELIGIOUS FREEDOM RESTORATION ACT

A 1990 US Supreme Court case, *Employment Division v. Smith*, made headlines. The case grew out of a situation in which two Native American drug rehabilitation counselors in Oregon were fired after it was discovered they had used the drug peyote as part of their traditional religious ceremonies. They were denied state unemployment benefits afterward and filed a lawsuit to receive them. Departing from some of its previous decisions on the free exercise of religion, the court ruled the Constitution did not give special protection to people who violated laws because of their religious beliefs. They would have to obey the law just like everyone else, even if it meant going against their religion, and even if the state interest behind enforcing the law wasn't that strong.

Strong public opinion arose against this particular ruling. Many religious groups saw the judgment as providing a way for the government to restrict unpopular religious practices. Rights groups all over the nation supported the passage of a new law, the Religious Freedom Restoration Act (RFRA). This law was intended to allow all Americans to practice their unique religious beliefs without government interference. President Bill Clinton signed the bill into federal law in 1993, although some saw it as an infringement on the Constitution's establishment clause.

The new law was tested in the 1997 case of *City of Boerne v. Flores*. The case involved a church in Texas that asked the city for permission to expand. The city denied the church's request, saying that the church was in a historic district and could not be altered. The church sued, citing their rights under the Religious Freedom Restoration Act. The city argued the RFRA was unconstitutional and did not apply. The Supreme Court agreed with Boerne and declared the RFRA could not be imposed on the states, although the federal law remained in effect. Since then, 21 states have passed their own versions of the RFRA. These laws are similar to, but not exactly the same as, the federal law.

A case involving a Texas church caused the Supreme Court to rule the federal Religious Freedom Restoration Act could not be imposed on the states.

CHAPTER THREE

A MATTER OF
CONSCIENCE

On the morning of December 16, 1965, in Des Moines, Iowa, 13-year-old junior high school student Mary Beth Tinker got dressed and went to school as usual. On that morning, she also wore a black armband to represent her feelings about US involvement in the Vietnam War (1954–1975). Her 11-year-old sister, Hope, and eight-year-old brother, Paul, and their 16-year-old friend Christopher Eckhardt did the same thing. They had decided to wear the armbands and fast on certain days during the holiday season as a way to express their deep sadness over the killing taking place in the war. The kids and their

Mary Beth Tinker and her brother John, who soon joined the protest, believed it was important to stand up for their right to protest in school.

parents, one of whom was a Methodist minister, had done this sort of thing together before and felt it was their duty to protest the horrific violence of war.

During the 1960s, demonstrations, marches, and protests over the war, the civil rights movement, and other social issues were commonplace. Many people felt strongly about these issues, and some were driven by religious beliefs, as the Tinker children were, to demonstrate their deep feelings of anger and frustration. Certain groups, including law enforcement, often saw these protesters as agitators, troublemakers, and rebels. Sometimes peaceful demonstrations turned violent and chaotic as tempers flared and protesters, government supporters, and police clashed. This sort of thing almost never happened in public schools, but school officials were wary of anything that might potentially cause trouble. As a result, most

"IT WAS THE SAME AS IF SOMEONE HAD WORN A CROSS AROUND THEIR NECK. LOTS OF PEOPLE HAD THE LITTLE CROSSES THEY'D WEAR. . . . IF THEY WERE GOING TO PROHIBIT US FROM WEARING AN ARMBAND, THEN THEY WERE GOING TO HAVE TO PROHIBIT KIDS FROM WEARING CROSSES TO SCHOOL BECAUSE THE ARMBAND WAS JUST SIMPLY AN EXPRESSION OF WHAT I BELIEVED."[1]

—MARY BETH TINKER DESCRIBING HOW HER RELIGIOUS BELIEFS LED TO HER DEMONSTRATION AGAINST THE VIETNAM WAR officials banned anything—signs, T-shirts, slogans, peace symbols, etc.—that might cause disruptions at school.

That was exactly what the principals of the Tinker and Eckhardt children's schools had done when they heard students planned to stage the black armband demonstration. They met with the Tinkers and Chris Eckhardt and strongly urged them not to take part, reminding them of the system-wide announcement that those who participated in an antiwar demonstration at school would be punished. The Tinker kids and Eckhardt discussed the situation among themselves and with their parents and decided they wanted to go ahead with their peaceful protest anyway.

When they arrived at school wearing the armbands, the kids were immediately sent to the principals' offices. The children were told to remove the bands, but they refused. Officials noted later that none of the children were angry, argumentative, or loud. In fact, they barely spoke at all, even though they were heckled and shouted at briefly by other students.

Mary Beth and Christopher were suspended from school on December 16, and John Tinker, Mary Beth's

15-year-old brother, was suspended for the same reason the following day. The two youngest Tinkers were not punished. Mary Beth, John, and Christopher remained suspended from school until after the Christmas break, when they returned to classes. They did not protest or wear armbands again, but they did wear black clothing for the rest of the school year, which was not against school rules.

That might have ended the story. But local news coverage about the kids' protest caught the attention of the American Civil Liberties Union (ACLU), a group that supports free speech and civil rights in a variety of ways.

The United States saw many antiwar demonstrations throughout the years of the Vietnam War.

The ACLU offered to fund a legal action, making a test case of a student's right to openly express a matter of conscience without punishment. The First Amendment to the Constitution granted citizens that right, but did the Constitution wording apply to schoolchildren as well? In 1968, that had not been decided. So ACLU lawyers helped the families file a lawsuit against the school system, claiming the students' constitutional right of free speech had been violated. The Supreme Court had already decided the term *free speech* did not only refer to vocal speech, but to written language and symbolic expressions, such as specific gestures, images, and colors that communicated a specific and clear idea or message that was generally understood by others. Black armbands certainly fit that description.

HAZARDOUS FREEDOM

The case known as *Tinker v. Des Moines Independent Community School District* proceeded through various lower courts until it reached the US Supreme Court in February 1969. The court justices found the students had, in fact, been unjustly denied their free speech rights. As the ruling stated: "The Constitution says that Congress (and the States) may not abridge the right to free speech. This provision means what it says. We properly read it to permit reasonable regulation of speech-connected activities in carefully restricted circumstances." The ruling also took note of the fact that the students "neither interrupted school activities nor sought to intrude in the school affairs or the lives of others. They caused discussion outside of the classrooms, but no interference with work and no disorder."[2]

The *Tinker* case fundamentally changed the way free speech cases involving students were dealt with in the courts. It also changed what students could say and do at school and how much teachers and principals could regulate

THE APPEALS PROCESS

The American judicial process allows the losing party in federal court cases to appeal. If the suit loses in a federal court of appeals, or in the highest court of a state, it may still be appealed. The losing party can file a petition for a writ of certiorari. This is a formal request asking the US Supreme Court to review the case. The Supreme Court does not have to review all cases sent to it for appeal. The justices usually choose to hear cases of particular public importance or ones they think deal with laws that need clarification. This is especially true when two or more lower courts have brought conflicting opinions or have interpreted a law differently. So the Supreme Court's purpose is to test and clarify confusing or vague laws and to give courts and law enforcement authorities guidance in how to apply them. The decision of the Supreme Court is final, and no further appeals are possible.

student speech and writing. Basically, the *Tinker* ruling said that unless it caused a "substantial disruption" to or "material interference" with the regular school routine, students were free to express ideas and opinions without fear of punishment.

Another important part of the *Tinker* decision was it meant that just because school authorities feared something bad might happen because of a student's actions or speech, this was not an acceptable reason to deny that student the right to act or speak. This meant officials had to have some real reason to suspect violence or disruption would occur if a student spoke or acted. This part of the ruling caused a great deal of confusion and frustration among educators in the years following *Tinker*. People wondered how anyone could know ahead of time what words or demonstrations might cause disorder. Critics particularly argued that when children's safety is at

"FIRST AMENDMENT RIGHTS, APPLIED IN LIGHT OF THE SPECIAL CHARACTERISTICS OF THE SCHOOL ENVIRONMENT, ARE AVAILABLE TO TEACHERS AND STUDENTS. IT CAN HARDLY BE ARGUED THAT EITHER STUDENTS OR TEACHERS SHED THEIR CONSTITUTIONAL RIGHTS TO FREEDOM OF SPEECH OR EXPRESSION AT THE SCHOOLHOUSE GATE."[3]

—JUSTICE ABE FORTAS, PRIMARY AUTHOR OF THE *TINKER* RULING, 1969 stake, it should always be best to err on the side of caution. Judge Abe Fortas, principal author of the *Tinker* ruling, answered such concerns by stating the US Constitution makes it clear that running such risks is part of living in a democratic society. In fact, he said, "This sort of hazardous freedom is the basis of our national strength."[4]

Even though other cases since 1969 have altered students' free speech rights, *Tinker* remains a landmark case, one frequently cited in support of other cases. After all, the courts had never before said that students had rights beyond those school officials were willing to grant them. That decision opened the door for a multitude of other types of challenges. Students have used it, for instance, to support their right to preach or spread a

The Tinker family, including mom Lorena, Paul, and Mary Beth, celebrate their victory in the Supreme Court.

religious message or printed material at school. Others have used the case as the basis for demonstrations for and against homosexuality, abortion, prayer in school, and other controversial issues.

The lesson of *Tinker* is not just that individual actions by people of all ages can have a huge impact. The case also illustrates just how vital a constant reinterpretation of the US Constitution is in a democratic society. Rights guaranteed in the First Amendment, particularly free speech and religion, must continually be fought for against all attempts to restrict or deny them.

T-SHIRT PROTEST

Tyler Harper objected to a demonstration a student group at his school organized. The April 2004 event was held to promote understanding and acceptance of LGBTQ (lesbian, gay, bisexual, transgender, or queer) students at the school. Similar to the Tinkers, Tyler showed his opposition by wearing his disapproval, in his case, a T-shirt emblazoned with the words, "Homosexuality is Shameful. Romans 1:27." When he refused to obscure the message or remove the shirt, authorities ordered him to leave the school building. Tyler sued, claiming his rights to free speech and free practice of his religious beliefs were denied. He cited the *Tinker* case as a precedent.

The court also cited *Tinker* in its decision in *Harper v. Poway Unified School District* (2006), but the justices chose to apply it a different way. Harper's rights had not been violated, the court ruled, because the school reasonably concluded wearing the T-shirt would be hurtful to gay and lesbian students and "interfered with their right to learn."[5]

FROM THE HEADLINES

BONG HITS 4 JESUS

The US Supreme Court ruling in *Morse v. Frederick* is often seen as closely connected with *Tinker*. The case grew out of a highly publicized incident at an Alaska high school in 2002. At an event taking place in front of the school, student Joseph Frederick displayed a 14-foot (4 m) sign with the words "Bong Hits 4 Jesus." The student later said he had no political or religious reason for displaying the sign, just that he wanted to test the limits of his right to free speech and to see what his principal, Deborah Morse, would do. What she did was immediately confiscate the sign, over Frederick's strong objections that by doing so she was violating his right to free expression. Morse saw the disturbance the sign might cause with its somewhat confusing message that appeared to celebrate and encourage drug use. Frederick, who was 18 at the time, was suspended for ten days.

Similar to the *Tinker* case, *Morse v. Frederick* traveled through the appeals process and landed in the US Supreme Court in 2007. The ruling handed down by a 5-4 majority was that school officials had a right to control expression that appeared to glorify drug use. This decision supporting schools' attempts to retain order reversed a tendency by the court ever since *Tinker* to rule in favor of student rights. Although a majority of justices reaffirmed the *Tinker* principle that students do not give up their free speech rights when they are in school or at school related

Students rallied to support Joseph Frederick and student free speech while the Supreme Court decided his case.

events, some justices worried about the court's willingness to make exceptions to *Tinker's* rule that student speech should be protected unless it created a "material disturbance."

CHAPTER FOUR

IN THE PUBLIC
SQUARE

T
he term *religious speech* means more than just someone standing behind a pulpit or on a street corner shouting religious ideas to attentive congregations or at oblivious passersby. As the *Tinker* case showed, free speech does not have to involve oral language at all. Simply displaying a color, symbol, sign, or shape that communicates an idea or belief is speech, too, protected under the First Amendment—or at least it is under some circumstances.

The practice of most major religions involves the display of certain symbols or images that convey great meaning and significance. For Christians, the cross is an important symbol. For Jews, the menorah, a seven- or nine-branched candleholder, and the Star of David are

The world's religions are represented by a variety of symbols, including, from top right, Islam, Hinduism, Buddhism, Judaism, and Christianity.

THE COVERED GIRL CHALLENGE

In April 2015, a group of students at a Cincinnati, Ohio, school suggested an event they felt would improve cultural and religious understanding in the school. Agreeing with their reasoning, the principal decided to allow the "Covered Girl Challenge" to take place. The idea was that girls in the school who wished to participate would wear a hijab, a traditional Islamic head covering, for a day at school to experience a small piece of Muslim culture.

What started as a voluntary exercise in cultural awareness quickly turned into an angry debate over free speech, bigotry, and religious freedom in public schools. The principal canceled the event after she began receiving angry phone calls and messages from parents and community residents. Some of the protests were anti-Muslim, arguing the school was using taxpayer money to promote Islam. Others thought it was making fun of religious stereotypes. Still others thought the challenge violated the separation between church and state, or they objected to the head coverings as symbols of female repression. But not everyone was against the event. A local leader in the Muslim community said, "to cancel something whose whole objective was to build understanding is extremely disappointing."[1]

highly meaningful. Although most symbolism and images are forbidden for Muslims, they still use the green star and crescent symbol to represent Islam on flags and signs. The mere presence of any of these and other sacred images may inspire feelings of reverence and devotion in believers of that faith. Many Americans feel it is their right to display them whenever and wherever they wish.

Yet, just as the First Amendment may restrict what a person may utter in certain places, it also may control when and where certain religious images are displayed. According to the US Constitution, the government must make no religious statements. To do so "establishes" one particular religion over another. That means publicly owned land or buildings, or the "public square," as it sometimes referred to, must remain open to any and all ideas, including religious ones, but never dedicated to just one. Publicly owned land or buildings must not display religious words or symbols in a way that suggests the government endorses those particular words or symbols.

In 1959, a local Catholic organization donated a religious statue to the city of Marshfield, Wisconsin. The white marble image was a 15-foot (4.5 m) statue of Jesus Christ standing with outstretched arms atop a large globe.

Some supporters of allowing religious displays in government spaces argue the US government has always had strong ties to Christianity.

Across the base of the statue were the words "Christ Guide Us on Our Way." The statue was placed in the city park on public property, clearly visible from the busy highway that passed nearby. For years, the park was a popular place for citizens to gather, play, and picnic.

In 1998, a local business owner and an organization called the Freedom From Religion Foundation (FFRF) sued the city, claiming Marshfield sponsored one religion over another. After all, they said, the city used tax money to pay workers to keep the public park and the religious statue in it clean and well maintained. Anyone who visited the park would reasonably assume the religious message represented by the large statue in that park was one the city government itself promoted.

The city promptly sold the statue and the small plot of land on which it stood to a citizens group that had quickly formed. The group took over maintenance of the monument and the small piece of park around it. Now the statue was on private land, not public. The FFRF and the local business owner appealed the decision to a higher court, which found the city still violated the First Amendment. Church and state were still not separate enough, since anyone who wandered into the park would still assume the city had erected the statue and supported its clearly religious message. The matter was not settled until the city of Marshfield built a large, permanent fence around the statue and erected a sign defining exactly where public land ended and private land began.

The case shows clearly how the Constitution works in making a distinction between public and private spaces. The city's fault was not that it allowed religious speech in a public space. The law does not forbid religious expression in public places, as long as it is orderly and peaceful. The

RELIGIOUS SIGNS IN FRANCE

France, unlike the United States and some other democratic nations, bans all conspicuous religious signs, from Islamic head scarves to Jewish skullcaps and Christian crosses, in public places. Since the controversial law went into effect in 2004, many religious groups have demonstrated against and sometimes attempted to defy the ban. Critics accuse France of curbing freedom of religious expression and forcing religious people to abandon centuries-old traditions. For the French government, however, the ban is only part of a century-long tradition of keeping private religious expression out of the secular public realm. The government has stated its intent was not to oppress religious practice, but to encourage people of all nationalities and faiths to live together in openness and harmony. Public places, particularly schools, are simply seen as religion-free zones. Many of France's millions of Muslims disagree. They see the ban as the government giving in to growing anti-Muslim feelings in France. Hundreds of women have been fined for ignoring the ban, although French police claim the law is rarely enforced.

problem in Marshfield was a Christian message was the only voice heard in the park. Had other religious and nonreligious groups been invited to erect images and symbols expressing their particular beliefs, no suit could have succeeded.

Yet religious speech and practice in public spaces is still going to be controversial. Inviting religions into the nonreligious public square means the one that shouts the loudest gets the most attention. If everyone gets to erect a monument, soon the public square is overcrowded, as each display tries to outdo the other.

COURTS IN CONFUSION

Disorder in the public square, as one legal scholar has noted, is often caused as much by the courts themselves as by religious groups clamoring for attention. Courts' interpretation and application of religious free speech laws over the years became difficult to predict. The reasons for this confusion are many and complicated. But perhaps the main reason has to do with the tendency for different officials and courts to understand and apply the same laws in different ways.

In a 2004 case, *Buono v. Norton*, a court of appeals ordered the removal of a World War I monument erected on federal land as a memorial to soldiers killed during the war. The eight-foot (2.4 m) cross was put up in a rugged part of Mojave National Preserve in California in 1934. It was difficult to reach, and few people saw it. A Buddhist group petitioned to place a shrine nearby and was denied. Frank Buono, a former assistant superintendent at the preserve, thought it was wrong that some religious symbols were allowed while others were denied, and he spearheaded a court case. Despite its remote placement, a federal court ruled in favor of those who wanted the cross

After a court battle, being covered in plywood, and being stolen, a new cross was rededicated on now-private land located within the Mojave National Preserve in 2012.

removed. People who might stumble upon the cross, they ruled, could assume the government had installed it as a religious statement, a clear violation of the establishment clause of the Constitution, the court said.

Congress attempted to transfer the plot of land to private ownership but a court blocked the move, saying it didn't resolve the constitutional problem. However, in 2010 the Supreme Court ruled the land transfer was allowed to go forward. A new cross was erected in 2012.

Almost at the same time, a Texas man sued the state government. He claimed a monument engraved with the Ten Commandments of the Old Testament on the grounds of the state capitol building was an unconstitutional government endorsement of religion. In the case of *Van Orden v. Perry*, a district court and a circuit court of appeals ruled against Van Orden. The

"THE GOAL OF AVOIDING GOVERNMENTAL ENDORSEMENT [OF RELIGION] DOES NOT REQUIRE ERADICATION OF ALL RELIGIOUS SYMBOLS IN THE PUBLIC REALM. . . . A CROSS BY THE SIDE OF A PUBLIC HIGHWAY MARKING, FOR INSTANCE, THE PLACE WHERE A STATE TROOPER PERISHED, NEED NOT BE TAKEN AS A STATEMENT OF GOVERNMENTAL SUPPORT FOR SECTARIAN BELIEFS."[2]

—JUSTICE ANTHONY KENNEDY, MAJORITY OPINION IN THE MOJAVE CROSS CASE, 2010

Supreme Court agreed with lower courts, stating the monument, which had been in place since 1961, was historically significant and, therefore, served a purpose other than a religious one. Any reasonable observer, the court said, would assume the religious words did not necessarily represent a government endorsement of any particular religion. In addition, the Texas capitol has many monuments dedicated to state history, which puts the Ten Commandments into a historical context instead of a religious one.

On the very same day, June 27, 2005, the court ruled on another case in which the Ten Commandments appeared on monuments and public displays at courthouses and schools in three Kentucky counties. In this case, *McCreary County v. ACLU*, the justices reached the opposite decision given very different facts. The Kentucky counties had said specifically the displays were intended to endorse religion. The Ten Commandments displays in Kentucky, the ruling said, were "undeniably a sacred text in the Jewish and Christian faiths," and their display in public spaces violated the First Amendment's rule against establishment of religion.[3]

FROM THE
HEADLINES

WEARING ONE'S RELIGION

What happens when the clothing one wears is a major religious statement? Problems especially occur when the clothing one's religion requires is in direct conflict with accepted standards of the public space in which it is worn.

Such situations have frequently arisen in recent years concerning the Muslim practice of girls and women wearing a head covering in public: the hijab, a kind of scarf that covers the head, neck and upper chest. In the United States, many public schools have set rules against students wearing any sort of head covering. Schools are somewhat different from other public places. Even though "students or teachers [do not] shed their constitutional rights to freedom of speech or expression at the schoolhouse gate," as the Supreme Court ruling in the *Tinker* case determined, schools can control what students say and do, if they have a reason to do so.[4] They can restrict behavior or speech if it is disruptive, dangerous, or may violate other students' rights— and if the rules are consistently applied to all students.

But different schools interpret the law differently. In a 2012 case, a Muskogee, Oklahoma, school suspended a Muslim student for continuing to wear a hijab to class after she was ordered not to do so. A US Department of Justice (DOJ) investigation revealed the school allowed other students to wear head coverings on certain occasions for nonreligious reasons. The department ruled the school had violated the girl's right to free religious practice and expression simply because she was a Muslim, a religion that was not popular. DOJ investigators called the school's actions "un-American and morally despicable."[5]

Some Islamic groups require women to cover more of their faces and bodies than others.

CHAPTER FIVE

GAY RIGHTS AND
FREE SPEECH

Phil Robertson, the scraggly bearded star of television's *Duck Dynasty*, was answering an interviewer's direct question. But Robertson's characteristically direct answer sparked a firestorm of controversy when it appeared in the January 2014 issue of *GQ*, the popular men's fashion magazine. The media, particularly online, exploded into a raging debate that touched on issues of free speech, religion, and conflicting beliefs.

Phil Robertson speaks before the Conservative Political Action Conference in 2015, accepting the group's award for defending the First Amendment.

The question that started the furor was this: "What, in your mind, is sinful?"[1] Anyone who has ever watched the show knows the family it features never hides its fundamentalist religious beliefs and practices. Particularly not Phil, a born-again Christian and self-proclaimed "Bible-thumper," who leads the Robertson clan in prayer at least once per episode and freely preaches his opinions about everything, including his commitment to God, country, and duck hunting.[2]

It was Robertson's answer to the sin question, however, that struck many people as simply going too far. When asked to define sin, Robertson answered, "Start with homosexual behavior and just morph out from there. Bestiality, sleeping around with this woman and that woman and that woman and those men." He also said that "homosexual offenders, the greedy, the drunkards, the slanderers, the swindlers—they won't inherit the kingdom of God." Presumably speaking for his family, he quickly added, "We never, ever judge someone on who's going to heaven, hell. That's the Almighty's job. We just love 'em, give 'em the good news about Jesus—whether they're homosexuals, drunks, terrorists. We let God sort 'em out later, you see what I'm saying?"[3]

Gay rights organizations, including GLAAD, quickly condemned the comments, saying that ideas like Robertson's encouraged "vile stereotypes" about gays and lesbians.[4] Blogs and social media were filled with demands for *Duck Dynasty* to be removed from the airwaves. A CNN commentator said, "Whatever the 'reasons' you have for being bigoted, at the end of the day, it's still bigotry. You can't hide behind 'it's my religious beliefs' as a justification for bad behavior."[5]

A&E, the channel that carried the reality series, needed to distance itself from the antigay comments, so it suspended Robertson from the show for several episodes. But many felt the punishment was not harsh enough, particularly after the Duck Commander returned to the show only a few episodes later.

"[PHIL] ROBERTSON DIDN'T FALSELY YELL FIRE IN A CROWDED THEATER—WHICH SUPREME COURT JUSTICE OLIVER WENDELL HOLMES JR. SAID WAS NOT PROTECTED BY THE FIRST AMENDMENT BACK IN 1919—SO HE IS LEGALLY FREE TO SAY WHATEVER HE WANTS . . . ABOUT ANYONE HE WANTS. BUT THAT DOES NOT MEAN HE IS PROTECTED FROM HOW PEOPLE REACT TO WHAT HE SAYS."[6]

—WRITER AND TV COMMENTATOR ELZIE "LZ" GRANDERSON

Supporters believe Robertson's right to free speech allows him to say anything he wants.

Many people did not agree with the sense of outrage others expressed over Robertson's remarks. Some of them wondered whether Robertson's comments were really so hurtful or whether the intensely negative reactions were exaggerated. As the Republican governor of Louisiana, Bobby Jindal, said, "I don't agree with quite a bit of stuff I read in magazine interviews or see on TV. . . . But I also acknowledge that this is a free country and everyone is entitled to express their views."[7] In February 2015, Robertson received the Andrew Breitbart First Amendment Award given by the Conservative Political Action Conference. The award, according to its sponsors, is meant to celebrate someone "who faces down the forces of secularism and political correctness and refuses to back down." In accepting the award, Phil Robertson said simply, "All of us ought to be able to speak freely."[8]

LGBTQ DISCRIMINATION

Members of the LGBTQ (lesbian, gay, bisexual, transgender, queer) community have been discriminated against for years. Only in the past couple of decades have they emerged as a unified and vocal political force on the national stage and demanded their full rights as citizens. The movement hit a high point in June 2015 with the Supreme Court ruling that the US Constitution protected the right of same-sex couples to marry.

SAME-SEX MARRIAGE

On June 26, 2015, in one of the Supreme Court's most historic rulings, the justices decided by a 5-4 majority that same-sex couples have a constitutional right to marriage. The ruling struck down bans in 14 states. The justices ruled that preventing same-sex partners from marrying violated their constitutional right to due process under the Fourteenth Amendment. The decision also found that the states were unable to present a compelling reason to withhold that right from people. The decision meant gay and lesbian couples would be able to marry immediately in the four states named in the case—Kentucky, Ohio, Tennessee, and Michigan. The Court's decision reflected growing support for gay marriage nationwide. An April 2015 poll conducted by ABC News and the *Washington Post* found 61 percent of those asked said gay and lesbian couples should be allowed to legally marry.[9]

Yet discriminating against people because of their sexual orientation is legal in many states. Employers can fire workers because of their sexual orientation. Landlords can refuse to rent to same-sex couples. There is no federal law banning discrimination against LGBTQ people in public accommodations, which include restaurants, hotels, and similar places, and less than half the states outlaw it.

Indiana's state legislature passed a controversial religious freedom bill in early 2015 that went into effect in July 2015. Indiana immediately became the target of critical reaction nationwide from those who feared its specific wording could allow members of certain religious groups to legally discriminate against LGBTQ persons. Supporters of the law argued it was never meant as an antigay law, but not everyone was convinced. After all, they said, the bill stated that state or local governments were

"WHETHER HOMOSEXUALITY IS MORAL OR IMMORAL IN AN ABSOLUTE SENSE IS NOT A MATTER FOR LEGISLATURES OR COURTS TO DECIDE. INSTEAD THE MANDATE OF COURTS IS TO PROTECT THE RIGHTS OF INDIVIDUALS TO MAKE MORAL ASSESSMENTS, UNLESS THE STATE CAN DEMONSTRATE SOME COMPELLING INTEREST IN THE OUTCOME OF SUCH ASSESSMENTS."[10]

—FROM *RELIGION ON TRIAL: HOW SUPREME COURT TRENDS THREATEN FREEDOM OF CONSCIENCE IN AMERICA*

After the initial passage of Indiana's RFRA, many businesses put up signs stating they would not discriminate.

prohibited from "substantially burdening a person's ability to exercise their religion—unless the government could show it has a compelling interest to do so and that the action is the least-restrictive means of achieving it."[11]

Many saw the original bill's wording, which differed slightly from the federal religious freedom law, as opening the door for discrimination of all kinds. It was possible to envision cases in which fundamentalist Christian business owners could refuse services for same-sex weddings—music, catering, flowers, clothing, or cakes. Same-sex partners feared the law could allow a private agency to refuse to allow them to adopt or serve as

foster parents, if the agency had moral objections to same-sex relationships.

Faced with continued criticism and billions of dollars in lost tourism profits, business and political leaders urged the government to correct the wording of the RFRA. Lawmakers responded by changing the wording of the law in mid-April to make it perfectly clear no business would be allowed to deny goods or services to LGBTQ people. Many did not feel the new wording went far enough. Still, a large number of gay and lesbian residents saw the efforts of leaders as a turning point. It seemed to signal a change, a growing tolerance for them in their community and nationwide.

The Episcopal Church is one religious group that supports same-sex marriage.

FROM THE
HEADLINES

WESTBORO BAPTIST: FREE SPEECH OR HATE SPEECH?

Even from 1,000 feet (300 m) away, the signs the protesters displayed were shocking. "God Hates America." "Thank God for 9/11." "Thank God for Dead Soldiers."[12] Even more disturbing was the occasion at which the demonstrators chose to display the signs—the 2006 funeral of a young soldier killed while fighting in Iraq. The protesters were from the Westboro Baptist Church in Topeka, Kansas. According to their leader, Reverend Fred Phelps, the purpose of the demonstration was to spread his church's main message that homosexuality is evil and God is punishing the United States for its tolerance of homosexuality. It did not matter, Phelps said, that the man whose funeral they were picketing was not gay. Protesting and demonstrating was practicing their religious beliefs, which under the First Amendment could not be restricted, he said.

The soldier's family sued the church for the emotional suffering their words and actions had caused. But in March 2011, the Supreme Court ruled the church did have the constitutional right to stage such protests. In his ruling, US Supreme Court Chief Justice John Roberts wrote:

Speech is powerful. It can stir people to action, move them to tears of both joy and sorrow, and—as it did here—inflict great pain. On the facts before us, we cannot react to that pain by punishing the speaker. As a Nation we have chosen a different course—to protect even hurtful speech on public issues to ensure that we do not stifle public debate.[13]

Two women kiss in a counterprotest in front of Westboro Baptist Church members.

CHAPTER SIX

SCHOOL PRAYER
AND BIBLE
READING

I n the late 1950s, at the beginning of every school day in New York's public schools, children were asked to recite a prayer written for them by their School Board of Regents. The prayer said, "Almighty God, we acknowledge our dependence upon Thee, and we beg Thy blessing upon us, our parents, our teachers and our country."[1]

In 1958, five families decided, each for separate reasons, that their children should not be exposed to the daily prayer. One of the parents, Steven Engel, called the recitation a "one-size-fits-all prayer that doesn't fit

In public schools, the line between student-led voluntary prayer and school-sponsored prayer can be difficult to define.

"ONE NATION UNDER GOD"

The reciting of the Pledge of Allegiance has been the subject of legal suits for years and continues to be a topic of controversy today. The issues, as seen in such cases as *Minersville School District v. Gobitis* (1940) and *West Virginia Board of Education v. Barnette* (1943), relate to whether students have the right to refuse to recite the pledge. The landmark Supreme Court decision in *Barnette* established that the First Amendment free-speech clause includes the right of students not to speak. So students do not have to recite, stand, or place hands over hearts if they chose not to.

Another First Amendment challenge to reciting the pledge has related to objections to the phrase "under God," added by Congress in 1954. Some people feel the phrase endorses a specific religion. Others feel the reference to God in the pledge is similar to its use in historical documents and government proceedings. Cases such as *Newdow v. U.S. Congress* (2000) and *Elk Grove Unified School District v. Newdow* (2004) make it clear the controversy over the pledge to the flag is far from over.

the religious faiths of all the people."[2] The families filed suit in federal court to stop the practice. The case, *Engel v. Vitale*, was the first-ever school prayer case to reach the Supreme Court. The court's 1962 ruling was that such a prayer in a public school is unconstitutional under the Constitution's establishment clause.

A firestorm of protest swept the nation. School districts that saw it as an attack on organized religion were outraged. One legal analysis noted, "It takes only a very minor prophet to predict that various forms of organized though non-denominational prayers will persist in our public schools."[3] Many school officials vowed to defy the court's order and continue prayer in their schools. Members of Congress and national religious leaders condemned the decision, too, calling it a victory for communism.

The lone dissenting vote in the court was Justice Potter Stewart. He argued that Americans "are a religious people whose institutions presuppose a Supreme Being." There are certain practices and institutions of government, he said, that are "deeply entrenched and highly cherished," and they were definitely not an example of the establishment of a state church.[4]

The Supreme Court was flooded with mail, most of it critical, some of it threatening. Cities and towns staged protest marches, mourning the loss of what they saw as a fundamental religious right. Not all of the reaction was negative. Many people at the time hailed the decision, such as one legal

"OF ALL THE ISSUES THE ACLU TAKES ON—REPRODUCTIVE RIGHTS, DISCRIMINATION, JAIL AND PRISON CONDITIONS, ABUSE OF KIDS IN THE PUBLIC SCHOOLS, POLICE BRUTALITY, TO NAME A FEW—BY FAR THE MOST VOLATILE ISSUE IS THAT OF SCHOOL PRAYER. ASIDE FROM OUR EFFORTS TO ABOLISH THE DEATH PENALTY, IT IS THE ONLY ISSUE THAT ELICITS DEATH THREATS."[5]

—MICHELE A. PARISH OF THE ACLU, QUOTED BY JUSTICE HARRY BLACKMUN RULING IN THE 1992 CASE OF *LEE V. WEISMAN* observer who said it was "a testament to the idea that government can't coerce anyone to take part in religious activity."[6]

One analyst has called *Engel* "a case that changed America." Perhaps a more accurate observation on *Engel* is one made by a writer who examined how the school district the Engel children attended had changed. In 1962, he noted, the city was nearly all white and primarily Catholic, Protestant, and Jewish. In 2008, he discovered half the population was Asian, and a local community index revealed the presence of 12 different religions. The local school 2008 calendar made reference to days important to the three religions present in 1962, and also acknowledged students who practiced Islam, Hinduism, and Baha'i. This would suggest, he concluded, "that *Engel* did not so much change America as prepare it for changes that were the inevitable result of other forces."[7]

"THIS VERY PRACTICE OF ESTABLISHING GOVERNMENTALLY COMPOSED PRAYERS FOR RELIGIOUS SERVICES WAS ONE OF THE REASONS WHICH CAUSED MANY OF OUR EARLY COLONISTS TO LEAVE ENGLAND AND SEEK FREEDOM IN AMERICA."[8]

—JUSTICE HUGO BLACK EXPLAINING WHY HE RULED AS HE DID IN *ENGEL V. VITALE*

READING THE BIBLE IN SCHOOL

The *Engel* school prayer furor had not yet died down when a year later, in 1963, the Supreme Court launched another bombshell. This time, ruling in the case of *Abington Township School District v. Schempp*, the court declared school-sponsored Bible reading and reciting the Lord's Prayer were equally unconstitutional.

The case was based on a complaint filed by a family who objected to a state law they said offended the belief and practices of their family's Unitarian religion. Their home state of Pennsylvania had a law that said: "At least ten verses from the Holy Bible shall be read, without comment, at the opening of each public

MURRAY V. CURLETT

A companion school prayer case heard with *Schempp* was *Murray v. Curlett*. The Murray in this case was 14-year-old William Murray, son of Madalyn Murray O'Hair. O'Hair was an outspoken champion of socialist and atheist causes who made herself the center of a whirlwind of controversy in the 1950s and 1960s. She promoted her intense antagonism against organized religion and what she saw as intrusions of religion in the secular world.

Madalyn Murray O'Hair encouraged her son to challenge a Baltimore, Maryland, school board rule first passed in 1905 that required each school day to begin with Bible reading or prayer. William first protested to school officials, then staged a symbolic strike, refusing (with his mother's blessing) to go to school for 18 days.

The Murrays' original lawsuit said the district's practice of forcing students to take part in Bible reading and prayer recitation violated William's rights as an atheist. The Murrays lost the lawsuit and appeals but won in the Supreme Court, consolidated with *Schempp*.

school on each school day."[9] The law stated any student would be excused from listening to or attending the Bible reading "upon the written request of their parent or guardian."[10] But the Schempps believed the act of removing themselves from the room every time the Bible was read unfairly singled children out for embarrassment and ridicule.

The court accepted the case to further define aspects of religious practice it believed had been overlooked in *Engel*—religious literature and other religiously oriented recitations. In their ruling, the justices noted the mere presence of the Bible in schools did not violate the law.

The Schempp family arrived at the Supreme Court to hear the verdict in their case.

Bibles could be used for purely secular purposes, such as the study of literature or along with other documents that supported good moral virtues. But the Bible could not be used as an instrument of religion, particularly not in ceremonies or rituals of a distinctly "devotional or religious character."[11]

In its *Schempp* ruling, the court attempted to clarify its motives in banning prayer and Bible reading from schools. Obviously, the justices had received a great deal of criticism. Much of it was based on the appearance that the court was attacking religious people and institutions. Using almost poetic language, Justice Tom C. Clark tried to point out that, in his opinion, by separating church and state, the court was actually protecting and elevating religion, not

THE RIGHT TO BE EXCUSED

A common defense schools have offered for continuing Bible reading and other overtly religious practices is they always allow students who do not choose to participate the right to be excused. In his *Schempp* ruling, Supreme Court Justice William Brennan called this situation "a cruel dilemma." He pointed out that peer pressure and the desire of every person to fit in makes it an extremely difficult and stressful thing for students to do. "Even devout children may well avoid claiming their right," he said, "and simply continue to participate in exercises distasteful to them because of an understandable reluctance to be stigmatized as atheists or nonconformists."[12]

attacking it: "The place of religion in our society is an exalted one, achieved through a long tradition of reliance on the home, the church and the inviolable citadel of the individual heart and mind." He concluded that "it is not within the power of government to invade that citadel, whether its purpose or effect be to aid or oppose, to advance or retard."[13]

These two cases did not end the debate about the place of prayer in schools. Through the 1980s and 1990s, the Department of Justice continued receiving complaints, and the courts continued hearing cases pertaining to prayers and the display of religious signs and images at school sporting events, assemblies, graduations, and other events.

The 2000 case of *Santa Fe Independent School Dist. v. Doe* is a recent ruling pertaining to school-endorsed religious activity. The case was complicated because it involved an assortment of religiously motivated activities supported by the Santa Fe, Texas, school and its employees. Among these were incidents in which teachers distributed religious information urging students to

Protestors supporting school prayer in Pensacola, Florida, in 2009 showed the debate over school prayer was far from settled.

attend local church meetings, and at least one event in which a student of a minority faith in the community was belittled and badgered by teachers and students over her beliefs.

The names of those who filed the suit against the Santa Fe system were withheld by request of the filers. The court used the name Doe on the official documents. The plaintiffs feared they and their children would be subjected to intimidation and violence "due to militant religious attitudes" in the school and community.[14]

Only one of the issues in the case reached the Supreme Court, concerning a student-led, pregame prayer presented routinely over a PA system at football games. The school district argued it did not appoint the students who prayed; other students elected them democratically. Since the school also did not influence what the students said, it was a free speech issue, not a religious one.

The court ruled the district had violated the law. The justices found the school's policies involved both perceived and actual endorsement of religion. After all, they permitted a pregame prayer and provided the equipment that amplified it so no one could escape hearing it. Holding elections to select the students who prayed was also incorrect, since it "turns the school into a forum for religious debate and empowers the student body majority to subject students of minority views to constitutionally improper messages."[15]

The local district court found it necessary a month after the complaint was filed to warn the Texas school district to stop extreme attempts to identify those who had filed the original suit. The court threatened the school with "the harshest possible contempt sanctions," and even criminal charges for their "intimidation and harassment," in trying to find out the names behind Doe on the case documents. The court particularly condemned bogus petitions, questionnaires, individual interrogation, and "downright snooping" in the school and community.[16]

"NOTHING IN THE CONSTITUTION AS INTERPRETED BY THIS COURT PROHIBITS ANY PUBLIC SCHOOL STUDENT FROM VOLUNTARILY PRAYING AT ANY TIME BEFORE, DURING, OR AFTER THE SCHOOL DAY. BUT THE RELIGIOUS LIBERTY PROTECTED BY THE CONSTITUTION IS ABRIDGED WHEN THE STATE AFFIRMATIVELY SPONSORS THE PARTICULAR RELIGIOUS PRACTICE OF PRAYER."[17]

—FROM THE SUPREME COURT RULING IN THE CASE OF *SANTA FE INDEPENDENT SCHOOL DIST. V. DOE*

EVOLUTION VS. CREATIONISM

For most Americans at the end of the 1700s, the biblical description of creation was the most plausible explanation for the diversity and complexity of life on Earth. The idea that a divine being had, some 10,000 years earlier, created all life in the exact form and function they existed in 1776 was accepted by the majority.

An alternative to the prevailing theory appeared with the 1859 publication of naturalist Charles Darwin's *On the Origin of Species*. What the book said was incredibly disturbing for many people. Instead of a single creation event as described in the book of Genesis in the Bible, Darwin outlined a force he called natural selection. This force, he said, produced gradual

In the book of Genesis in the Bible, the first two humans, Adam and Eve, live peacefully in the Garden of Eden with every type of animal.

Darwin's theory of evolution by means of natural selection changed science and religion forever.

change, or evolution, over millions of years, resulting in the

diversity and complexity of life. Not only had it happened,

Darwin said, it was still happening. Creation was an

ongoing process.

For many people, Darwin's ideas seemed to be an

attack on their most deeply held beliefs about God and

the truth of the Bible. Yet by the mid-1920s, discussion of

Darwinian evolution was included in most public school

science textbooks. As a result, a movement supported

by fundamentalist Christian groups began opposing the

teaching of evolution in US public schools. In the 1920s, several states passed antievolution laws, and free speech groups, such as the ACLU, began legal efforts to stop them.

The Scopes Monkey Trial of 1925 was a highly publicized case staged, initially, by the ACLU. They arranged the trial as a way to test the constitutionality of a Tennessee antievolution law, the Butler Act. Teacher and coach John Scopes agreed to be tried on the charge of illegally teaching evolution. The trial, which drew intense national attention, has always been widely viewed as a debate between two contrasting ideas: creationism and evolution. And both sides did play up that idea. In reality, the trial was really something of a formality. Everyone involved understood from the beginning that the event was only a first step in an appeals process that would lead to the Supreme Court. In that high court, the real issue—whether state laws banning the teaching of evolution were constitutional—would be decided.

When Clarence Darrow and William Jennings Bryan, two towering figures of their day, volunteered to join the trial on opposite sides, the media hype took over. Bryan was an immensely popular political figure and orator.

MORE TO THE STORY

THE BOOK BEHIND THE SCOPES MONKEY TRIAL

It may be surprising to learn that William Jennings Bryan did not oppose the teaching of evolution in public schools. In fact, he agreed with much of Darwin's theory—as it applied to fish and frogs. What he could not believe was that humans had evolved from lower life-forms, especially monkeys. That popular misunderstanding of human evolution is how the famous trial got its name.

What troubled Bryan and others even more than human evolution was the overall point of the textbook used in Tennessee, *Civil Biology* by George Hunter. The author urged students to study human biology as a civics lesson. Hunter claimed that, through evolution, the Caucasian race had become superior to all others. Hunter compared people of lesser races to pests that must be controlled. Good world citizenship, Hunter suggested, would require the white race to act on these principles, so undesirable species might be weeded out and mankind would continue to evolve upward. This hateful idea, known as eugenics, has been responsible for the horrors of slavery and Nazi extermination camps during World War II (1939–1945). Bryan and other religious leaders of the 1920s fought bitterly against eugenics, and this was no doubt one reason he agreed to come to Tennessee. He wanted to be part of a case that might get Hunter's warped vision of mankind thrown out of schools.

Darrow was perhaps America's most famous trial lawyer and a self-proclaimed atheist. His main goal was to ridicule Bryan and his religious views and turn public opinion in favor of evolution.

Thousands of people, including hundreds of reporters from all over the country, flocked to tiny Dayton, Tennessee, to witness the event. WGN radio in Chicago, Illinois, even aired live broadcasts from the courthouse. Because of the searing July heat, some of the hearings were held outdoors. In the end, the eight-day trial featured a great deal of bantering, but little of substance was said or settled.

The trial provided enough legal fireworks to satisfy most spectators. But ultimately, the Scopes Trial did not accomplish what the ACLU had hoped. When the *Tennessee v. Scopes* case reached the state Supreme Court, the justices refused to rule on the case. Instead, they declared the case a mistrial. The judge in Dayton, they said, had not followed proper legal procedure when he ordered Scopes to pay a $100 fine, when he should have allowed the jury to set the amount. Thus, Tennessee's ban on

teaching human evolution in schools remained in effect, as it did in many other states and cities, for the next 40 years.

Despite its failure as a test case, the Scopes Trial was still an important moment in American culture and thought—"the most important trial of our age," according to legal analyst Carl S. Kaplan. Legal professor Douglas O. Linder agrees. The trial, he said, "was about something important, something that's still important—the conflict between religion and science and whether the two can be reconciled."[1]

In 1968, the Arkansas Education Association decided to challenge its state's antievolution law, even though no teacher had ever been charged with violating it. Science teacher Susan Epperson volunteered to represent Arkansas teachers in the case to test the constitutionality of the state law. A lower court first ruled the state law restricted free speech and tried to establish a particular religion by silencing the teaching of an unpopular idea. The state Supreme Court overturned that ruling. It claimed the state had a right to determine what could and could not be taught in its schools. But the US Supreme Court

Clarence Darrow, *right*, and John Scopes, *center*, with cocounsel Dudley Field Malone, *left*, failed to get evolution accepted into the Tennessee school curriculum.

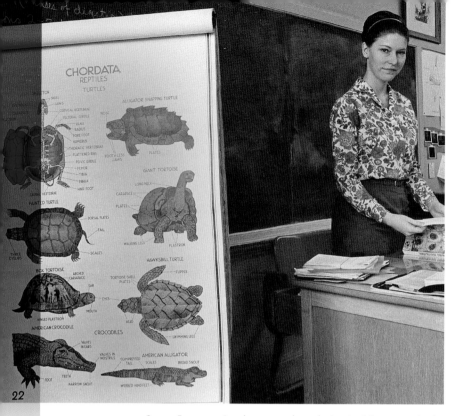

Susan Epperson fought to teach evolution in Arkansas schools.

agreed with the lower court. In *Epperson v. Arkansas*, the court ruled state bans on teaching evolution clearly violated the First Amendment. The state had passed the law specifically because evolution was "deemed to conflict with a particular religious doctrine; that is . . . a particular interpretation of the Book of Genesis by a particular religious group."[2] In his ruling, Judge Abe Fortas wrote that the "First Amendment does not permit the State to require that reading and learning must be tailored to the principles or prohibitions of any religious sect or dogma."[3]

The *Epperson* case didn't solve every situation in every state, however. Twenty years later, the teaching of evolution came to the attention of the US Supreme Court again. This time, the court heard the case of *Edwards v. Aguillard.* The case dealt with a law passed in 1981 in Louisiana that required schools to teach a balanced treatment of both evolution and creation science. By adding the word *science,* the state could claim the purpose of the law was not purely religious, as had been the case in *Epperson,* but was in the spirit of academic inquiry, to present students with both sides of the scientific debate and let them decide for themselves.

In *Edwards v. Aguillard,* the Supreme Court once again ruled that while the idea of academic fairness was a good one, creation science "embodies the religious belief that a supernatural creator was responsible for the creation of mankind."[4] Teaching this in any form was still a matter of government establishing a specific religion, which the First Amendment to the Constitution banned.

Neither Supreme Court ruling ended the controversy over teaching evolution or creationism in schools, however. One local school board in Georgia attempted to

NOT JUST AN ORDINARY CITIZEN

The 1994 case of *Peloza v. Capistrano Unified School District* was a reverse of the usual evolution complaints filed in federal courts. In this case, a biology teacher brought suit against his school district based on the requirement that he teach evolution as part of the regular curriculum. The school also ordered him not to discuss his religious beliefs with students. Peloza claimed the first requirement was a violation of the establishment clause since evolution is "a religious belief system" in conflict with his own. The second requirement, he said, was a violation of his rights of free religious practice and free speech. The court ruled, "The Supreme Court has held unequivocally that while the belief in a divine creator of the universe is a religious belief, the scientific theory that higher forms of life evolved from lower forms is not." The court also ruled that a teacher speaking about his religious beliefs "is not just any ordinary citizen" and the "likelihood of high school students equating his views with those of the school is substantial."[6] To permit him to discuss his religious beliefs with students during school time on school grounds clearly violated the establishment clause of the First Amendment.

get around the law by placing stickers on students' biology books. The stickers read: "Evolution is a theory, not a fact, regarding the origin of living things. This material should be approached with an open mind, studied carefully, and critically considered."[5] A federal judge ruled the stickers had to be removed since, by speaking negatively about evolution, they clearly represented the local school's endorsement of the opposite view, which is a religious one.

The most recent attempts to insert creationism into curricula involve the term *intelligent design*. The idea behind intelligent design is an attempt to address what critics say are gaps in Darwin's theory. According to intelligent design theorists, life is far too complex to have been the result of random evolution over millions of years. An intelligent mind must have been there at the beginning to make it all happen.

In 2004, the Dover Area School District in central Pennsylvania attempted this approach. The textbook it adopted for biology classes taught evolution. But teachers were also required to introduce students to a contrasting viewpoint by reading a statement. It said in part: "Because Darwin's Theory is a theory, it continues to be tested as new evidence is discovered. The Theory is not a fact. Gaps in the Theory exist for which there is no evidence. . . . Intelligent Design is an explanation of the origin of life that differs from Darwin's view."[7] The school board also made available reference copies of an intelligent design book,

"IF A TEACHER IN A PUBLIC SCHOOL USES RELIGION AND TEACHES RELIGIOUS BELIEFS OR ESPOUSES THEORIES CLEARLY BASED ON RELIGIOUS UNDERPINNINGS, THE PRINCIPLES OF THE SEPARATION OF CHURCH AND STATE ARE VIOLATED AS CLEARLY AS IF A STATUTE ORDERED THE TEACHER TO TEACH RELIGIOUS THEORIES."[8]

—RULING OF THE SEVENTH CIRCUIT COURT OF APPEALS IN *WEBSTER V. NEW LENNOX SCHOOL DISTRICT, 1990*

Of Pandas and People, and encouraged students to read it in addition to their textbooks. The school board argued that the approach was adopted "for the secular purpose of improving science education and to exercise critical thinking skills."[9]

A group of local parents sued, and the federal court case *Kitzmiller v. Dover* went to trial in 2005. As the first case to test a school district policy requiring the teaching of intelligent design, the trial attracted national and international attention. Both plaintiffs and defendants in the case presented expert testimony over six weeks from September 26 through November 4, 2005. On

The United States is home to more than a dozen museums presenting creationist views, including this one in Kentucky.

December 20, 2005, Judge John E. Jones issued a ruling in which he said intelligent design was, after all, a form of creationism. Therefore, "it is unconstitutional to teach [it] as an alternative to evolution in a public school classroom."[10] Despite the ruling, local and state authorities still have tried to install creationism into school programs. In 2013, Missouri attempted to enact two separate intelligent design bills, both of which failed.

The results of a 2014 Gallup poll perhaps show why the fight over evolution in schools is almost certainly not over. The poll revealed approximately 42 percent of Americans believe God created humans in their present form 10,000 years ago, a view that has changed little in the past three decades. The survey also showed people living in the South, what is commonly known as the Bible Belt, are more likely to believe in creationism than are people living in other regions. This is also why, as a Gallup poll explains, efforts "to have creationism addressed in the public schools might be an important political issue in that region."[11]

THE
DIGITAL AGE

I t's easy to imagine Thomas Jefferson and James
Madison firing tweets back and forth during
arguments over what should be in the new
Constitution. Benjamin Franklin was a scientist,
diplomat, inventor, and a dozen other things. Imagine
what his website and blog would have been like. If he
had text messaging, YouTube, and Facebook, he would
have almost certainly used them. But, of course, none
of the Founding Fathers, even in their wildest dreams,
could have foreseen smartphones, cyberspace, the
cloud, or any of the other techno-digital miracles we
casually take for granted today. Yet, somehow, when
they wrote the US Constitution, they had to construct
a set of legal guidelines specific enough to cover the

The Internet requires the Constitution to evaluate situations the
Founding Fathers never could have imagined.

"THERE ARE MORE THAN THREE HUNDRED MILLION WAYS IN WHICH AMERICANS EXPRESSING THEMSELVES MIGHT GIVE OFFENSE TO THOSE WHO MAKE IT THEIR BUSINESS TO BE OFFENDED. IS THE WHITE HOUSE GOING TO PUT EVERY AMERICAN CRANK ON SPEED-DIAL SO IT CAN TELL THEM TO SHUT UP WHENEVER A MOB GATHERS OUTSIDE A US EMBASSY OR CONSULATE?"[1]

—EDITOR AND JOURNALIST LEE SMITH, SPEAKING ABOUT THE IMPOSSIBILITY OF CONTROLLING CYBER AND DIGITAL MESSAGES

situations they could visualize but vague enough to deal with those they could not.

Today's law enforcement, government officials, and courts are faced with a whole new array of legal situations that must be sorted out within the confines of a document written more than 200 years ago. Schools struggle, too, as they try to figure out how the First Amendment applies to issues such as cyberbullying, hate speech on student blogs and Facebook, and the rights of student journalists. Where does reasonable oversight stop and censorship begin?

The *Tinker v. Des Moines School District* (1969) case is still one of the legal precedents most often cited in cases related to the free speech rights of students. Another is *Hazelwood School District v. Kuhlmeier*, a 1988 Supreme Court case that mainly dealt with student journalists.

Student staff members of the school newspaper filed the complaint that was the basis of *Hazelwood* after their principal removed three stories from an issue before it went to press. They claimed the principal had violated their First Amendment rights. The Supreme Court ruled the students' free speech rights were not violated in this case because the newspaper was written in a journalism class as part of the requirements of that course. The class was part of the school's regular curriculum and served an educational function; therefore, it was not a public forum open to anyone who might want to use it to express an opinion.

Principal Robert Reynolds displays the issue of the school newspaper that sparked the *Hazelwood* court case.

CENSORSHIP VS. THE RIGHT TO RECEIVE

Several Supreme Court cases have confirmed the First Amendment "right to free speech" guarantee protects the "right to receive information and ideas" for minors as well as for adults. In one particular case, *Board of Education v. Pico* (1982), the Supreme Court ruled that school officials in New York violated the First Amendment by removing several books from junior high school library shelves because they did not agree with the ideas in them. The court said the First Amendment "does not permit the official suppression of ideas."[3]

But the debate over censorship in schools and elsewhere in society has not ended. The opinions of the justices in the *Pico* decision were varied and confusing. They offered no clear guidelines for schools or courts to follow. One aspect that is still argued is whether the *Pico* decision relates to things other than printed books.

The *Hazelwood* ruling is still used more than 20 years later in cases dealing with students' use of school computers. School officials often use *Hazelwood* to argue they can censor student expression if the school has a reasonable educational reason for doing so. The ruling also made students who use school computers subject to their schools' Internet policies. Still, as *Tinker* made clear, school officials can only restrict a student's right to free speech if they reasonably suspect that offensive speech will cause a "substantial disruption" or "material interference" with school activities or "invade the rights of others."[2]

Yet, as legal analysts are finding, neither ruling fits every situation—particularly ones dealing with the

Internet and social media. School shootings, such as those at Columbine High School in Colorado, Sandy Hook Elementary in Connecticut, and Virginia Tech in Virginia, have forced schools to become much more watchful of threatening things students might post online or write in class.

One such situation occurred in Nevada in the mid-2000s. Students at a Nevada high school became alarmed when a student began sending graphically violent text messages to friends. Over the course of several months, the boy bragged about his collection of guns, including a semiautomatic weapon. Friends knew he actually did own such weapons, so they worried when his profane and graphically threatening messages began naming certain teachers and students at school.

The boy's friends finally told a teacher and the principal, who in turn notified police. The boy was not arrested, but the school did suspend him for ten days in 2008. He was also temporarily expelled. The boy and his parents sued, claiming that since the boy was not in school at the time of the postings, his free speech rights had been violated. Their attorney also cited the *Tinker* case ruling, stating that the school could not prove the boy's speech had "substantially disrupted" school proceedings.

The court disagreed. In 2011, the judge found the boy's violent messages, which graphically threatened the safety of everyone at his school, had made it reasonable for school officials to assume a substantial disruption of school activities might occur. The boy's punishment was upheld.

A somewhat similar case, *Burge v. Colton School District 53* (2015), involved a middle school student who used his home computer to post hateful entries aimed at a teacher. When other students told her about the posts, the teacher

In some situations, schools can intervene when students make comments online outside of school, but not always.

became frightened, and the principal punished the boy with three days of in-school suspension. The boy and his parents sued the school, charging officials with violating his free speech rights since he was not in school at the time he posted the comments. The boy's lawyer argued that, just as in *Tinker*, the student's actions had caused no "substantial disruption" in school proceedings. The teacher had missed no work or suffered any ill affects from fear. This time, the court agreed the school had violated the student's free speech rights.

INTERNET REGULATIONS

Issues pertaining to the Internet, particularly how and if it should be regulated and controlled, are still being discussed and debated today. In the United States, one of the first major attempts to control what children and students might encounter online was the Communications Decency Act (CDA), passed by Congress in 1996. Among other things, the law attempted to stop the spread of online pornography and other obscene material and also control hateful language on blogs and websites. But neither item was defined clearly enough. The Supreme

Court decided only a year later that the CDA violated the First Amendment's guarantee of freedom of speech.

In their ruling on the case of *Reno v. American Civil Liberties Union* (1997), the justices recognized the Internet is far different from other forms of communication, both written and broadcast. They also agreed that laws previously used to regulate written and broadcast media did not apply to the types of digital issues people faced online. In 2000, Congress passed the Children's Internet Protection Act (CIPA), which states K-12 schools and

While the First Amendment protects free speech on the Internet in the United States, other countries including China censor their citizens' access to online content.

libraries in the United States must use Internet filters and other measures to protect children from harmful online content. It was signed into law on December 21, 2000.

The American Library Association (ALA) immediately challenged the law as an unconstitutional restriction of free speech rights. But in 2003, the Supreme Court ruled the CIPA was constitutional. The ruling stated that the need to protect "young library users from material inappropriate for minors is legitimate, and even compelling."[4] Since then, libraries that receive federal funds must provide minors with computers containing software programs that filter

FILTERING AND THE LIBRARY BILL OF RIGHTS

Organizations such as the ACLU and the ALA believe people of all ages have the right to access the Internet. In fact, the ALA argues that the First Amendment guarantees that right, despite the fact that the Supreme Court ruled the Children's Internet Protection Act constitutional in 2003. The ALA's "Library Bill of Rights" emphatically states, "A person's right to use a library should not be denied or abridged because of origin, age, background, or views." It also declares, "Books and other library resources should be provided for the interest, information, and enlightenment of all people of the community the library serves."[5]

The Brennan Center for Justice at NYU School of Law, a free speech, anticensorship institute, expressed similar reservations about filtering software in their "Free Expression Policy Project" report in 2006. The report referred to filtering devices as "sweeping censorship tools" and saw their use as "a pressing public policy issue to all those concerned about free expression, education, culture, and democracy."[6]

out pornography and other objectionable materials. Adult users are still permitted to use unfiltered computers.

THE FIRST AMENDMENT AND SOCIETY

The First Amendment to the Constitution guarantees Americans an incredible richness of privileges—"inalienable rights," as the Declaration of Independence calls them. US government is based upon the recognition that these rights are inherent in each person and can never be taken away or violated. Laws set the limits of these rights, and our governmental system monitors the laws so no individual can claim more privilege than any other individual.

But, as Irish orator John Philpot Curran once said, "The condition upon which God hath given liberty to man is eternal vigilance."[7] In other words, along with the privilege of living in a free society comes the responsibility to monitor, guard, and test the laws that are the framework of democracy. The judiciary system and

"THE HISTORY OF CENSORSHIP SHOWS THAT IT IS COMPLETELY USELESS IN STAMPING OUT IDEAS: THE FASTEST WAY TO SPREAD AN IDEA IS TO CENSOR IT."[8]

—POLITICAL ANALYST NAOMI R. WOLF

98

legislatures do this, but so do individual citizens. The Supreme Court is the ultimate judge of what the law means. Yet, at the center of every case that comes before that body is a person trying to work out his or her own concept of what freedom means.

The amazing constitutional machinery established by the Founding Fathers more than 200 years ago still works today, perhaps better than they could have imagined. A main cog in that machine is the delicate balance between church and state. The Constitution fully recognizes that freedom of religion must be a key element in a democratic society. But to ensure society's continuation, religion must be monitored by a secular government, one that does not dictate any particular belief. As Jefferson said, the wall that separates church and state must stand as a solid and impenetrable barrier.

ESSENTIAL
FACTS

MAJOR EVENTS

- The Scopes Monkey Trial (1925) pits evolution against creationism in the courts.

- *Engel v. Vitale* (1962) proves school-initiated prayer violates the First Amendment.

- The *Tinker v. Des Moines* (1969) case rules students do not leave their rights at the schoolhouse door.

- On January 7, 2015, murders at the *Charlie Hebdo* offices in Paris, France, push questions of religious freedom versus free speech into the headlines.

KEY PLAYERS

- America's Founding Fathers, the framers of the US Constitution, understood the importance of setting up a democratic system of laws strong enough to ensure everyone's rights, yet pliable enough to allow for future interpretation.

- The US Supreme Court, a panel of nine judges, is empowered by the Constitution to interpret and clarify the law. The court hears cases dealing with controversial issues or issues of prime importance to the nation.

- Founded in 1920, the American Civil Liberties Union (ACLU) is one of America's most active participants in supporting the constitutional rights of citizens. The ACLU has sponsored many of the landmark cases heard by the Supreme Court.

IMPACT ON SOCIETY

Many of the rights Americans cherish most, and sometimes take for granted, are guaranteed in the First Amendment of the Constitution. These include the rights to free speech, to assemble peacefully, and to practice religion (or not to) without government force or interference. Life in the United States would be very different if these rights were not exercised and strenuously protected.

QUOTE

"The place of religion in our society is an exalted one, achieved through a long tradition of reliance on the home, the church and the inviolable citadel of the individual heart and mind. . . . It is not within the power of government to invade that citadel, whether its purpose or effect be to aid or oppose, to advance or retard."

—*Justice Tom C. Clark, ruling in* Abington Township School District v. Schempp

GLOSSARY

AMENDMENT

A change or addition to a law, bill, or constitution.

ATHEIST

One who does not believe in God.

BIGOTED

Strongly disliking certain people or ideas, without reasonable cause.

BLASPHEMY

Any speech or action that mocks or insults God or his representatives.

CENSORSHIP

The suppression of ideas and information that certain individuals, groups, or government officials find objectionable or dangerous.

EVOLUTION

A gradual change; Charles Darwin's theory that life on Earth arose from simple organisms and that genetic processes, such as mutation and natural selection, led over millions of years to the complexity observable in nature today.

FORUM

A place for public discussion or debate.

FUNDAMENTALIST

Relating to a Protestant Christian religious movement centered on a literal interpretation of the Bible.

INTELLIGENT DESIGN

A form of creationism based on the assumption that man, nature, and the universe contain clear evidence that a supernatural being (God) was involved in their creation.

PLAINTIFF

A person who sues another person or organization or brings legal action.

PRECEDENT

Something that comes before; a decision made at some earlier time by a legal court or authority that becomes a standard used to support a later claim, case, or decision.

ADDITIONAL
RESOURCES

SELECTED BIBLIOGRAPHY

Blakeman, John. *The Bible in the Park: Federal District Courts, Religious Speech, and the Public Forum*. Akron, OH: U of Akron P, 2005. Print.

Dupre, Anne Proffitt. *Speaking Up: The Unintended Costs of Free Speech in Public Schools*. Cambridge MA: Harvard UP, 2009. Print.

Hamilton, Marci A. *God vs. the Gavel: The Perils of Extreme Religious Liberty*. New York: Cambridge UP, 2014. Print.

FURTHER READINGS

Haynes, Charles C., Sam Chaltain, and Susan M. Glisson. *First Freedoms: A Documentary History of First Amendment Rights in America*. New York: Oxford UP, 2006. Print.

Lusted, Marcia Amidon. Tinker v. Des Moines: *The Right to Protest in Schools*. Minneapolis: Abdo, 2013. Print.

WEBSITES

To learn more about Special Reports, visit **booklinks.abdopublishing.com**. These links are routinely monitored and updated to provide the most current information available.

FOR MORE INFORMATION

For more information on this subject, contact or visit the following organizations:

Newseum Institute's First Amendment Center
555 Pennsylvania Avenue NW
Washington, DC 20001
202-292-6100
http://www.newseuminstitute.org
Located between the White House and the US Capitol, the Newseum allows visitors to explore historic artifacts, photographs, interactive exhibits, and more.

The Supreme Court
1 First Street NE
Washington, DC 20543
202-479-3030
http://www.supremecourt.gov/visiting/visiting.aspx
Visitors to the Supreme Court Building are encouraged to take advantage of a variety of programs during their visit, including courtroom lectures, an educational film, and various exhibits.

SOURCE
NOTES

CHAPTER 1. ALWAYS A RIGHT?
1. Carla Seaquist. "Free Speech vs. Responsible Speech: We Need to Talk, Again."
Huffington Post. Huffington Post, 3 Feb. 2015. Web. 29 July 2015.

2. "Charlie Hebdo Attack: Three Days of Terror." *BBC News*. BBC News, 14 Jan. 2015. Web.
29 July 2015.

3. Lisa Abend. "Free Speech Debate 'Still Alive' after Attack in Denmark." *Time*. Time,
14 Feb. 2015. Web. 29 July 2015.

4. Ashley Fantz. "Array of World Leaders Joins 3.7 Million in France to Defy Terrorism."
CNN. CNN, 12 Jan. 2015. Web. 29 July 2015.

5. Ed Payne. "France Bans Protests; Lebanese Demonstrators Call U.S. 'Enemy of God.'"
CNN. CNN, 19 Sept. 2012. Web. 29 July 2015.

6. "Muslim Press Reacts to Charlie Hebdo." *Radio Free Europe Radio Liberty*. Radio Free
Europe Radio Liberty, 9 Jan. 2015. Web. 29 July 2015.

7. Michael J. Totten. "Radical Islam's Global Reaction: The Push for Blasphemy Laws."
World Affairs. World Affairs, Jan/Feb 2013. Web. 29 July 2015.

8. William J. Gorta. "'Draw Muhammad' Contest Shooting: Two Suspects Dead, Guard Shot
in Texas." *NBC News*. NBC News, 3 May 2015. Web. 29 July 2015.

9. Adam Goldman, Craig Whitlock, and Marice Richter. "One Texas Suspect Was Accused in
2010 FBI Terror Case." *Washington Post*. Washington Post, 4 May 2015. Web. 29 July 2015.

10. "Landmark Cases: *Schenck v. US*." *PBS: The Supreme Court*. Educational Broadcasting
Corporation, 2007. Web. 29 July 2015.

11. "*Chaplinsky v. New Hampshire*, 315 US 568 (1942)." *Legal Information Institute*. Cornell
University, n.d. Web. 29 July 2015.

CHAPTER 2. THE ROOTS OF FREEDOM IN AMERICA
1. Julia Mitchell Corbett. *Religion in America*. Upper Saddle River, NJ: Prentice-Hall, 2000.
Print. 21.

2. Thomas Jefferson. *Notes on the State of Virginia*. London: John Stockdale, 1787. 265.
Google Book Search. Web. 29 July 2015.

3. "The Constitution of the United States: A History." *National Archives Charters of
Freedom*. National Archives, n.d. Web. 29 July 2015.

4. "Bill of Rights." *National Archives Charters of Freedom*. National Archives, n.d. Web.
29 July 2015.

5. Thomas Jefferson. "Letter to the Danbury Baptists (1802)." *Library of Congress*. Library
of Congress, n.d. Web. 29 July 2015.

6. Robert Barnes. "Supreme Court Upholds Legislative Prayer at Council Meetings."
Washington Post. Washington Post, 5 May 2014. Web. 29 July 2015.

7. Cathy Lynn Grossman. "'So Help Me God' Isn't in Official Presidential Oath." *USA Today.* USA Today, 17 Jan. 2013. Web. 29 July 2015.

8. "*Everson v. Board of Education of the Township of Ewing*, 330 US 1 (1947)." *Legal Information Institute.* Cornell University, n.d. Web. 29 July 2015.

9. "Religion and the Founding of the American Republic; Religion and the Federal Government, Part 1." *Library of Congress.* Library of Congress, n.d. Web. 29 July 2015.

10. Julia Mitchell Corbett. *Religion in America.* Upper Saddle River, NJ: Prentice-Hall, 2000. Print. 28.

11. Ibid. 27–28.

CHAPTER 3. A MATTER OF CONSCIENCE

1. Joseph Russomanno. *Speaking Our Minds: Conversations with the People behind Landmark First Amendment Cases.* Mahwah, NJ: Lawrence Erlbaum, 2002. Print. 11.

2. "*Tinker v. Des Moines Independent Community School District*, 393 US 503 (1969)." *Legal Information Institute.* Cornell University, n.d. Web. 29 July 2015.

3. Ibid.

4. Ibid.

5. "*Harper v. Poway Unified School District 20*, US Court of Appeals Ninth Circuit, 2006. *Findlaw.* Findlaw, n.d. Web. 29 July 2015.

CHAPTER 4. IN THE PUBLIC SQUARE

1. Hannah Sparling. "What Mason High's Hijab Battle Tells Us," *Cincinnati Enquirer.* Gannett, 19 Apr. 2015. Web. 29 July 2015.

2. "*Salazar, Secretary of the Interior, et al v. Buono*, 599 US 700 (2010)." *Findlaw.* Findlaw, n.d. Web. 29 July 2015.

3. "*McCreary County v. American Civil Liberties Union of Ky*, 545 US 844 (2005)." *Justia US Supreme Court.* Justia, 2015. Web. 29 July 2015.

4. "*Tinker v. Des Moines Independent Community School District*, 393 US 503 (1969)." *Legal Information Institute.* Cornell University, n.d. Web. 29 July 2015.

5. Marci A. Hamilton. *God vs. the Gavel: The Perils of Extreme Religious Liberty.* New York: Cambridge UP, 2014. Print. 65–67.

CHAPTER 5. GAY RIGHTS AND FREE SPEECH

1. Drew Magary. "What the Duck?" *GQ.* Condé Nast, Jan. 2014. Web. 29 July 2015.

2. Daniel Worku. "Duck Dynasty: Free Speech and Religion vs. LGBT Rights." *Liberty Voice.* Guardian Liberty Voice, 19 Dec. 2013. Web. 29 July 2015.

3. Drew Magary. "What the Duck?" *GQ.* Condé Nast, Jan. 2014. Web. 29 July 2015.

4. Catalina Camia. "'Duck Dynasty' Star Receives Free Speech Award at CPAC." *USA Today.* USA Today, 27 Feb. 2015. Web. 29 July 2015.

5. Breeanna Hare. "'Duck Dynasty' Reactions Debate: Free Speech or Bigotry?" *CNN.* CNN, 19 Dec. 2013. Web. 29 July 2015.

6. LZ Granderson. "'Duck Dynasty' Star's Free Speech Rights Weren't Violated." *CNN.* CNN, 20 Dec. 2013. Web. 29 July 2015.

7. Breeanna Hare. "'Duck Dynasty' Reactions Debate: Free Speech or Bigotry?" *CNN.* CNN, 19 Dec. 2013. Web. 29 July 2015.

8. Catalina Camia. "'Duck Dynasty' Star Receives Free Speech Award at CPAC." *USA Today.* USA Today, 27 Feb. 2015. Web. 29 July 2015.

9. Audrey Taylor, Arleta Saenz, and Mike Levine. "Same-Sex Marriage: Supreme Court Rules in Favor, President Obama Calls It 'Victory for America.'" *ABC News.* ABC News, 26 June 2015. Web. 29 July 2015.

10. Phillip E. Hammond, David W. Machacek, and Eric Michael Mazur. *Religion on Trial: How Supreme Court Trends Threaten Freedom of Conscience in America.* New York: AltaMira, 2004. Print. 123.

SOURCE NOTES
CONTINUED

11. Tony Cook. "Gov. Mike Pence Signs 'Religious Freedom' Bill in Private." *IndyStar.* Gannett, 2 Apr. 2015. Web. 29 July 2015.

12. Lindsay Deutsch. "Five Incendiary Westboro Baptist Church Funeral Protests." *USA Today.* USA Today, 21 Mar. 2014. Web. 29 July 2015.

13. "*Snyder v. Phelps et al,* 562 US __ (2011). *Findlaw.* Findlaw, n.d. Web. 29 July 2015.

CHAPTER 6. SCHOOL PRAYER AND BIBLE READING

1. Rob Boston. "Awesome Anniversary: Engel At 50: NY Families Ended Coercive Prayers in Schools." *Church & State* 65.6 (2012). 15. *MasterFILE Premier.* Web. 29 July 2015.

2. Peter Irons. *God on Trial: Dispatches from America's Religious Battlefields.* New York: Viking, 2007. Print. 28.

3. "*Engel v. Vitale.*" *New Republic* 147.2, Issue 2488 (9 July 1962): 4. Print.

4. Anne Proffitt Dupre. *Speaking Up: The Unintended Costs of Free Speech in Public Schools.* Cambridge MA: Harvard UP, 2009. Print. 165.

5. Ibid. 163.

6. Rob Boston. "Awesome Anniversary: Engel At 50: NY Families Ended Coercive Prayers in Schools." *Church & State* 65.6 (2012). 15. *MasterFILE Premier.* Web. 29 July 2015.

7. Thomas Healey. "The Battle over School Prayer: How *Engel v. Vitale* Changed America." *Political Science Quarterly* 1 Mar. 2008. Print. 179–180.

8. "*Engel v. Vitale,* 370 US 421 (1962)." *Legal Information Institute.* Cornell University, n.d. Web. 29 July 2015.

9. "*Abington School Dist. v. Schempp,* 347 US 203 (1963)." *Findlaw.* Findlaw, n.d. Web. 29 July 2015.

10. Ibid.

11. Ibid.

12. Ibid.

13. Ibid.

14. Anne Proffitt Dupre. *Speaking Up: The Unintended Costs of Free Speech in Public Schools.* Cambridge MA: Harvard UP, 2009. Print. 195.

15. "*Santa Fe Independent School District v. Doe,* 530 US 290 (2000)." *Legal Information Institute.* Cornell University, n.d. Web. 29 July 2015.

16. Anne Proffitt Dupre. *Speaking Up: The Unintended Costs of Free Speech in Public Schools.* Cambridge MA: Harvard UP, 2009. Print. 195–196.

17. Ibid. 194.

CHAPTER 7. EVOLUTION VS. CREATIONISM

1. Carl S. Kaplan. "Rounding Up the Century's Greatest Trials Online." *Cyber Law Journal.* New York Times, 15 Oct. 1999. Web. 29 July 2015.

2. Anne Proffitt Dupre. *Speaking Up: The Unintended Costs of Free Speech in Public Schools.* Cambridge, MA: Harvard UP, 2009. Print. 198–199.

3. "*Epperson v. Arkansas,* 393 US 97 (1968)." *Legal Information Institute.* Cornell University, n.d. Web. 29 July 2015.

4. "*Edwards v. Aguillard,* 482 US 578 (1987)." *Oyez Project.* IIT Chicago-Kent College of Law, n.d. Web. 29 July 2015.

5. Laura Parker. "School Science Debate Has Evolved." *USA Today.* USA Toda, 28 Nov. 2004. Web. 29 July 2015.

6. "*John E. Peloza v. Capistrano Unified School District,* US Court of Appeals Ninth Circuit, 1994." *Talk Origins Archive.* Talk Origins Archive, n.d. Web. 29 July 2015.

7. Marci A. Hamilton. *God vs. the Gavel: The Perils of Extreme Religious Liberty.* New York: Cambridge UP, 2014. Print. 170–171.

8. "Clarifying the Legalities." *Understanding Evolution For Teachers.* University of California Museum of Paleontology, n.d. Web. 29 July 2015.

9. Marci A. Hamilton. *God vs. the Gavel: The Perils of Extreme Religious Liberty.* New York: Cambridge UP, 2014. Print. 171.

10. Peter Irons. *God on Trial: Dispatches from America's Religious Battlefields.* New York: Viking, 2007. Print. 317.

11. Frank Newport. "In US, 42% Believe Creationist View of Human Origins." *Gallup.* Gallup, 2 June 2014. Web. 29 July 2015.

CHAPTER 8. THE DIGITAL AGE

1. Michael J. Totten. "Radical Islam's Global Reaction: The Push for Blasphemy Laws." *World Affairs.* World Affairs, Jan./Feb. 2013. Web. 29 July 2015.

2. "Frequently Asked Questions—Speech." *First Amendment Center.* Vanderbilt University and the Newseum, n.d. Web. 29 July 2015.

3. "*Board of Education v. Pico,* 457 US 853, 853 (1982)." *Findlaw.* Findlaw, n.d. Web. 29 July 2015.

4. "*United States v. American Library Association,* 539 US 194 (2003)." *Legal Information Institute.* Cornell University, n.d. Web. 29 July 2015.

5. "Library Bill of Rights." *American Library Association.* American Library Association, 2015. Web. 29 July 2015.

6. Marjorie Heins, Christina Cho, and Ariel Feldman. "Internet Filters: A Public Policy Report." *Free Expression Policy Project.* Brennan Center for Justice at NYU School of Law, 2006. Web. 29 July 2015.

7. Suzy Platt. *Respectfully Quoted: A Dictionary of Quotations.* United States: Barnes & Noble, 1989. 200. *Google Book Search.* Web. 29 July 2015.

8. Naomi Wolf. "The Fastest Way to Spread Extremism Is with the Censor's Boot." *Guardian.* Guardian News and Media, 7 Apr. 2015. Web. 29 July 2015.

INDEX

ABOUT THE
AUTHOR

Michael Capek lives in northern Kentucky with his wife and two children. He is the author of numerous articles and books for young readers, including (from Abdo) *The Civil Rights Movement*, *Stonehenge*, and *The D-Day Invasion of Normandy*. A former English and journalism teacher, Michael spent 27 years teaching in public schools and dealing firsthand with many of the issues described in this book.